The Hat City after Men Stopped Wearing Hats

The Hat City after Men Stopped Wearing Hats

John Surowiecki

WINNER OF THE 2006 WASHINGTON PRIZE

THE WORD WORKS

WASHINGTON, D.C.

Acknowledgments

Agnieszka's Dowry: "The Italian Woman Upstairs." *Alaska Quarterly Review*: "What Her Door Said (after Catullus)." *Broken Bridge*: "J.Z. in Love." *Caduceus*: "The Wisest Aunt, Telling the Saddest Tales"; "I Dreamed I Was Drinking Manhattans with Frida Kahlo." *Chachalaca Poetry Review*: "Americanization of a Poem by Wislawa Szymborska." *Common Ground Review*: "Senior Citizens without Air." *Connecticut Review*: "Mrs. Tencza Standing Naked in Her Driveway"; "S.Z. Home from Vietnam (1968)"; "The Angel of Death Returns to New Haven." *Cumberland Poetry Review*: "Barfly Briefly Noted." *Emily Dickinson Awards in Poetry Anthology* (2002): "The Men in Marge's Life." *Folio*: "Raising Children in Time of War (1943, 1967, 2003)." *Freshwater*: "Matin No. 2." *Gargoyle*: "Watching *Sea Hunt* with J.Z. and S.Z."; "French Lesson (*après* Larry Rivers)." *Ginger Hill*: "My Backyard Celebrates the Pope's Birthday." *GW Review*: "Dog without a Larynx." *Indiana Review*: "For D., Who Enjoyed Reading Mystery Novels." *Kimera*: "The Polka King's Funeral (1963)." *Mochila Review*: "Connecticut Invaded by Praying Mantises (1950)." *Nimrod International Journal*: "Ariel"; "Matin No. 1 (Heroin Addict)." *Poetry*: "Mr. Z. Late in Life and Early in the Day"; "The Hat City after Men Stopped Wearing Hats"; "What I Know about Epistemology." *Rosebud*: "Death, Cocktails, St. Kitts." *Tar Wolf Review*: "A Solitary Plum and a Line from *Paterson*." *West Branch*: "Imaginary Seascape with Literary Orphans." *Wild Goose Poetry Review Web*: "The Childless Couple's Child." *Wisconsin Review*: "The Don Giovanni of Women's Shoes." *Xanadu*: "Shostakovich."

"The Hat City after Men Stopped Wearing Hats" was chosen by the Poetry Foundation for broadcast as part of its **Poem of the Day** program.

A number of these poems appeared in the chapbooks, *Bolivia Street* and *Dennis Is Transformed into a Thrush*. "Ariel" and "Barfly Briefly Noted" appeared in the chapbook, *Caliban Poems*.

I'd like to thank the members of the world's best writing group—Denise Abercrombie, Jon Andersen, Jim Coleman, Joan Joffe Hall, Ann Leventhal, Alison Meyers and David Morse—for their wisdom and support. Also, my thanks to: Debbie and Mike DeSantis, Brian and Lisa Fitch, Greg Ford, Terry Rentzepis, Marilyn Johnston, and Lonnie Black.

For Al and Dorothy Rodosevich
and, as always, Denise

CONTENTS

- | -

- ‖ -

- ||| -

I

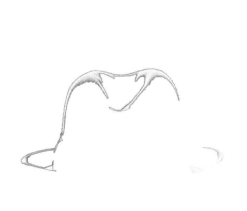

Connecticut Invaded by Praying Mantises (1950)

Neither DDT nor the stings
and poisons of other insects
had any effect on them.

They ate their young, pulled
hummingbirds out of the sky
and, if we dawdled or were

inattentive on our way
to school, they could paralyze
or kill us with a single bite.

And yet: if any of us were
ever lost and happened
to come upon one of them,

all we had to do was notice
which way it was pointed
and follow that direction home.

Connecticut Invaded by Chinese Communists (1951)

Through our basement window I saw
the world as a worm might or a cricket
or the dead. I thought there must be
a hole in the earth that began in China

and came out at last into our midnight,
under our stars, where only my mother's
Big Boys and black tulips stood between us
and their ruthless, mole-faced men.

I thought their bayonets would smell
of meat gone bad and feel like fire going
through me. My blood would accumulate
in small pools, forming small rivers,

and bullets entering my brain would
empty it of dreams, of children
with holes in their heads all ready to be
hooked up and yanked out of life.

Black Tulips

Disease twisted Olek's body and gave
him the strength of two grown men.

He dragged us into one end zone,
then the other, then back again, then

in circles perilously close to the beds
where my mother's tulips slept.

The whole time he howled and snorted
and nearly choked from laughing.

His father came by just before dark
and thanked us for being so kind to his son.

When Olek died that spring, the tulips
were holes you could look through,

as if the world were a movie screen
hiding an emptiness behind it, not night

or space, which were only darknesses,
but a parallel world of nothing at all:

and it was childish and wishful to
pretend it wasn't there. It was there.

And no one lived there. And no one
waited there for anyone.

Watching *Sea Hunt* with J.Z. and S.Z.

For now, we're in the gray waters
of what could be the Red Sea.
Framed portraits of Mrs. Z. are
given places of honor on shelves
and end tables along with holy cards
and laminated copies of her obituary
intended for use as bookmarks.
It's only a matter of time before
one of us begins to cry.

There's another earth and all it's
asked to carry is the weight
of oceans. Life is cold and silvery
and, farther down, the random spasms
of sunless light; but at least death isn't
attended by priests or dumbstruck
aunts or humorless men
with pike eyes and ballpoint pens
whose vigil will last as long as we live.

We wonder where we can get
goggles like that and waterproof
watches that glow in the dark
and tell the time in Alexandria
or if we can grow rubbery skins,
force-feed air into our lungs,
become, in fact, another species,
finned and mute, left alone
in a world as revealing as fog.

Strontium 90

Sifted out of clouds like all-purpose flour,
it finds its way into bones via textbook arrows
that point to rain, grass, a milk-producing cow
and a milk-drinking girl who looks a lot like you.

You tell me that compassion, which I admire in you,
is a form of helplessness, which I hate in myself,
and that dying as one is not so terrible as dying
one at a time. You tell me that our marrow
will melt and that all we can expect from our

last days are paradoxes: how we won't think
about love ever again and yet will think about it
all the time and how death will no longer exist
once we leave no one and nothing behind.

I, Fruit Fly

You were a sophomore,
now you're a planet
and I, your Sputnik,

pass summer nights
above the brown mythless
constellations of your skin.

I have two heads now
and two backs and wings
adorned with compound
eyes that see only you.

I have no mouth and my
children, who can only
be more monstrous and
confused, won't speak for me.

My years are your hours
and by the time I learn
what it means to remember,

there's nothing to recall,
nothing to tell me I was ever
anything to you.

French Lesson (*après* Larry Rivers)

She's asleep: *nez, menton, sein, vagin, genou, cheville,*
and *pied* in her hothouse house. All that wet
heat for a single palm—her *Le Douanier*—
crying, if it could cry, for Madagascar: lemurs,

chameleons, the Indian Ocean chasing sticks
like a *chien.* A shoot appears, a dagger straight-
up, another finger. *Eh quoi! tout est sensible?*

She reads about the Empire in its *décadence,*
about contumacious poets wringing the neck
of eloquence and Balzac declining hashish
at the Hotel Pimodan, curiosity, by Baudelaire's

account, at odds with self-control. She's *belle,*
I'm *bete.* She's an artist; she goes to Antioch.
And now she's up: *brillant, capricieux, bon.*

J.Z. in Love

He's no longer interested in Bondo-
ing his brother's piece-of-crap Chevy
or becoming one of the he-men in
his weightlifting magazines, hairless

and glistening like glazed doughnuts
and so bulked up their heads appear
absurdly small. He belittles the world
with courtesy, buffeted by the souls of lovers

who forever crisscross the earth, sharing
an implacable loyalty and fierce patience.
In an ordinary fly he finds an emerald.
Moonlight turns the world into an x-ray

of itself, daybreak washes away doubts
and regrets and in an instant he's talking
about oatmeal. He smiles a lot now: for
no apparent reason and for anyone to see.

S.Z. Home from Vietnam (1968)

He uses his Zippo without the wrist-flicking flourish
the rest of us still admire and he's already begun
the first of the hundred great novels every intelligent
person is expected to have read. He's suspicious

of those who are against the war: they come from
well-to-do families and care only about themselves;
and yet, the people he grew up with, people like him,
people like us, seem so eager to send him off to die.

He talks about the lives society has reserved for him,
lives no one ever wishes for or dreams of. When he
says he wants someone to expect great things of him,
we don't know what he means. We see him on the library

steps reading and smoking: the books look as if they're
on fire. He says reading is his insurance against ever
getting caught again with his dick exposed and with
no other option than waiting for someone to shoot it off.

II

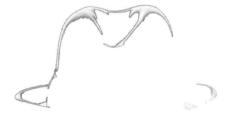

The Hat City after Men Stopped Wearing Hats

At the inauguration no one wore hats, not even
the poet whose hair the wind shaped into a fin.
We sat at the kitchen table trying to figure out
how we would make a living now that the river
no longer flowed carrot-orange to the Sound.

We used to tell the children that its fish wore
fedoras and suffered from mercury shakes,
twitching, lurching, losing scales as we would hair.
Every street used to be a river of hats and when
a war was won a sea of hats would suddenly appear.

Every day we'd walk to work leaning into the wind,
hands on our hats, and never once did we think
the factory doors would close and never once
did we notice the frost late on the lawns
like an interlude in a slaughtering of moths.

Thumbing through a 1974 Hartford Phone Book

1. White Pages

The columns of type form a ragged skyline
and in one of them her name is revealed
in a band of light from old detective movies;

the others are the heads she once turned
turned to names, names of the dead
or nearly dead by now, therapists and healers
among them, specialists in grief who gave

her small white pills and a room behind
the institute's quaint brick walls, insisting
she was only young and never doomed.

2. Yellow Pages

The cheese shop is gone, so is the Greek
restaurant on Asylum Street where listless
waiters danced listlessly; so is the art cinema

where sewers in *The Third Man* opened like tulips,
where life in *Vivre sa vie* was a terrible weight,
as if the sky were not only gray but made
of lead, and where she wondered why beautiful

young heroines always had to die—why
they just couldn't leap out of the brittle, dust-
edged frame and move to somewhere else.

The Angel of Death Returns to New Haven

In memory: Keane Callahan

The angel of death who placed the weight
of the world upon your helpless heart now asks
for our forgiveness, thinking he might have made

a terrible mistake taking you as early as he did,
not realizing what a good and principled man
you were and how the world would become
duller and cheaper and more brittle without you.

He drops by when we're clearing out a spot
for your tomatoes, a balding man in Bermuda
shorts who asks if he can bring us coffee
and crullers or maybe pick up a few things

at Home Depot; and when he has nothing more to say,
he blinks and blinks and blinks and blinks,
holding back the tears the world has yet to see.

What Her Door Said (after Catullus)

She left with someone you weren't smart
enough to suspect: most liars are bad liars

but good liars like her, because they shine
so brilliantly, also give themselves away.

What you thought was delight was only unrest.
She's thinking of going back to school.

She's thinking of losing weight.
She doesn't think of you.

Outside her new door is a vietnam
of dragonflies; maples have turned yellow

and goosenecks orange-soda orange. Stuck
in her vanity mirror is the image of a saint

who washed her skin with lime because
her beauty was too terrible to behold.

She's already dumped him and while she's
pregnant by you—it won't be for long.

Shostakovich

The plumbers say his music can flush sorrow
from a house or quench a thirst or right a life.

It walks their streets, following the spur tracks
where their children like to play, crawling up

derelict stairs like a local drunk; but mostly
it's the accompaniment to their long fixed stares

into a doily's web or a wallpaper's floribunda
or at the photo of a dead mother or a soldier

with his sleeve carefully pinned up or a new
couple dressed in uncomfortable new clothes.

Operetta

At the end of the street, there's a hill
of hearts and every week or two at least
one of the three Zajac girls tosses another
on the pile. They all live in an operetta
and sing arias about the never-ending
pleasures of being lovely and adored.

They've saved their stricken mother,
blinding Death with their beauty and charm
and locking him in a pantry filled
with canned goods—which is why
in mid-January, their myrtle blooms

in driveway shadows and the blue
earths of hydrangeas reappear with
small orange butterflies falling from
the heavens to seek them out. Now
their winter nights are our June nights,
thick with the aftershaves of young men

who gather in choruses and wonder
if it's grander to die of love than live
for love, straining for a glimpse of one
of the girls and seeing instead a man
eating peas at the pantry window.

The Don Giovanni of Women's Shoes

Lasciar le donne? Pazzo!

For him, love isn't the love of lovely things,
nor does it long platonically for the good,
nor is it only commerce,

the forced smile, the slight bow,
the gray suit, the occasional boutonniere;
for him, love is paying attention.

His thumb and forefinger are calipers
that measure the distance from one ankle
to the other. He slips his palm under her heel,

the callused floor of her life, then eases
her foot into the shoe until he hears
the escape of displaced air, a little sigh.

Knowing silence doesn't resonate
in a woman's heart, he praises what can
be praised, never forgetting to explain

discounts and warranties. He takes in
as much money as he can, but touches it
as if it were the stony hand of the dead.

The Italian Woman Upstairs

Chi piange? Io no, credimi.
—Salvatore Quasimodo

She tells us her son had lived for only a week,
then finds him in a stack of photographs,
dressed in a white linen smock, his face lost
in the shadow of a white bonnet. And so:

she won't drink milk or eggnog or eat
popcorn wrapped in red or green cellophane,
she won't touch embroidery or white satin
or gold leaf and she won't make raviolis

because they have chubby faces
with expressions you can never quite discern
and, straining for air, they get torn open
and fill the world with snow.

The Childless Couple's Child

Every now and then she dies of leukemia
or is carried away by chocolate waters.
Sometimes she's a blur under pond ice
or in their arms when their jet falls from the sky.

In all this time she's spoken a dozen words,
their words, but in a breaking, desperate voice:
utterances of incalculable loss, the tragedy
brought home, a sense of what it must be like.

She's always lighter than they remember
and frailer and more bashful, never asking
if she'll be given a name or a place in their hearts
or if there's ever been anyone else.

Imaginary Seascape with Literary Orphans

They've lived through novels
as bleak as a merchant's soul,
harassed by beadles and spinsters

who don't think they should smell
like manure or cheap pipe tobacco
or roam the tidewater claiming

hips for tea and clams for broth
and telling people to kiss their
royal orphan asses. They know

about winter seas that murder
in a minute, captains who sell
babies by the pound, shanghai

artists with eyes like the bubble
of a carpenter's level. They dream
of sailing to some island where

they'll find no word for themselves
and where nothing has more value
than someone's cold indifference.

Mr. Krok with a Wasp in His Ear

We have all the character and habits of the wasp.
—Aristophanes

Mr. Krok is a prick and a son of a bitch
and my father is delighted to hear him howl in pain.
It's only out of uncommon decency that
he rushes to help him, staring into his ear
as if the Crab Nebula were at the other end.
Another neighbor has called an ambulance,
but the wasp has already vanished into
the plum-colored evening and so has Mr. Krok.
My father suggests finding other insects and sticking
them into Mr. Krok's various other orifices,
but then a dragonfly accommodates his eye
and rests, a moth begs for light at his screen door
and a yellow jacket that would, if it were noon
and hot, drown in his drink, calls it a night instead.

Mr. Z. Late in Life and Early in the Day

He drains and coils the garden hose, done
shadowboxing with his most gigantic
and golden self. For the next hour or two
he deadheads lilies, recalling weddings
in shoreline towns where trees exploded
bud by bud and the ocean was as green

as a lime and clouds were as white as
a manager's shirt, where young people
were so casual about their claim over him,
their superiority and genius, making light
of his sad gratitude, his spot between

existing and exiting, his color, the color
of a pearl or the moon seen through
a cheap telescope. He scatters crystals
into the darkest heart of his oldest garden
where Mrs. Z. is whole again and lovely,

strolling past blackboard menus and bar
umbrellas, looking for him and the dead
they share, the young couples in brown
photos peeling from black pages, each
with an eager smile and a roll of fingers
curling like an early morning wave.

Mrs. Wrubel's Blueberry Pie

My friend is home from a state where they don't
grow blueberries. Here, his mother's bushes are
already rigged with netting and thick with fruit.

When she brings his pill, she brings him pie.
The filling is darker than her darkest iris.
Her secret, he says, is to use lard and plant

a handful of raw berries among the cooked.
We ask for seconds and, to feel her hands
dig deep into his shoulders, he asks for thirds.

In the fall, catbirds and robins feed freely
on her grapes. Of no interest to her, he says,
since there's no such thing as a grape pie.

Mrs. Tencza Standing Naked in Her Driveway

How thin she looks, like a girl, with tiny breasts
and scapulae the shape of turnovers sticking out
of her back, how her lips tremble as she sweats,

a living map of rivers: what we take to be her
pale complexion is only a layer of baby powder.

The police cover her with a blue blanket and speak
politely to her and to us, but all we can give them
are a few basic facts: she works in a bank,

her husband has been dead for years, she likes
giving neighborhood children jam-hearted candies.

My mother tells them that sorrows guide every life
like an atlas, but they're not interested and give her
a timid salute as they slam their car door forever shut.

The Men in Marge's Life

One liked her kamikazes and mojitos
and surprised her with nighties and mules.
One, an electrician, wound her life around his
as he would wire around his arm. One
had one nipple. One thumbed the moon

out of the sky as if it were a lozenge in a silver
wrapper and placed it at her feet. One provided
examples but never explanations as to why love
becomes unborn in a misappropriation of time.

One let her basil go to seed and her peonies
go flowerless; and in a snapshot she took,
one is his own ghost, double-exposed and half
cigarette smoke, floating above the first
unshoveled morning of our last hard winter.

The Polka King's Funeral (1963)

They liked that his casket was lined with robin's-
egg-blue satin undulating in G-clef patterns
and that his golden initials, so cleverly intertwined
and flecked with stars and Saturns and grace-
noted comets, once again blazoned from his pocket;
most of all, they liked that he kept his fez.

He had played at all their weddings, started
them on all their journeys, all bound for the same
unremarkable place, all the same to him.
He had given them a day of joy and frenzied music,
a day without bosses or angry looks or remarks
about being poor or uneducated or just plain stupid.

In return, they gave him a joyless hour and, heads
bowed, they sang their sluggish hymns.

My Backyard Celebrates the Pope's Birthday

The bird-cherry, the horseradish
and the spirea are surprises
of airy, sweet-smelling, aspirin-

white flowers: a snowfall in May.
The lilacs speak eleven languages;
the sparrows teach by existing.

Violets surround themselves
with children. Lilies of the valley
withstand a tyranny of cold.

The tulip tree is a yellow whisper,
the tulip a palsied hand; and there,
my dying cat naps in quattrocento light.

Dog without a Larynx

A given day has its given torments:
trucks, chain saws, children somewhere,
blackbirds shrieking in the heat of day.
Even a cardinal, a quart of blood in a tree,
can drive her nuts with its love calls.

She has a camera's eye, an unerring ear,
never a culpable heart. Relationships
collapse, helixing down to compassion;
hearts mend soon enough; cancer can be
defeated by acts of will and imagination.

It's perfectly quiet there now. Her dog
came back in September, squeaking
and hissing at everyone, not much of
a guardian against our neighborly concern
or the intruder not even she can hear.

Ariel

His death was not unlike that of any other servant,
not unlike the way a housecat finds its end
at the end of its last circle or a canary falls
a few inches to reach its place in heaven.

His freedom was a dizziness that never stopped;
there was no one left to delight and charm,
no one to tell him what to say and what to do.
He died looking out a window, a spirit

who became a ghost, who couldn't shut off
his invisibility. His masques and clever songs
come to mind, as do his electrical storms;
but he was best known for his obedience.

The Sadness Associated with Crab Lice

Now that I'm their geography,
I wonder if they have a history,
a flag, a national anthem, a Latin
motto, an ancient homeland
other than your sister's culottes.

They infest my dreams, scuttling
out of a calm full sea to claim
an endless forest of branchless trees,
a continent of warm hospitable meat.

Your shampoo will reduce them
to a few brown crystals half-hidden
in the folds of your twice-boiled sheets:
for you, the precipitate of regret;
for me, the debris of love.

I Dreamed I Was Drinking Manhattans with Frida Kahlo

1

The city marvels at her recklessness
and tolerance for unceasing pain.
And she's taken with its elephant-

gray skin and the way shadows move
from one side of its streets to the other,
reminding her of the phases of the moon.

A golden age is translated into glass boxes
and inside them the charity of bartenders
is unwavering. She keeps telling them:

No, there isn't a second universe for artists,
just the one and everyone has to live in it.

2

She talks about boys who play football in
stadiums made of dust; shoeless, their feet
never touch the ground. This is what happens

when you live in a hole in a map. You float
above the pigs and chickens, you argue
the child's position, a champion of wonder.

You fly to the mountains, green hands
holding blue lakes, and are astounded at
how dense the forest roof is and how dark.

All you see is a faraway light, an insect of light,
a blinking eye of light, the light of a minor star.

3

We are two assassins planning the death
of an afternoon that doesn't exist. Everyone
dreams of her because her face is everywhere.

Her eyes are onyxes, her hair onyxspun;
her skin is the color of her drink, the blood of
and release from suffering. She listens for

jaguars, monkeys, tuxedoed orchestras.
She airs out her thighs and says: *My friend,
it's time for a toast.* And so we raise our glasses:

*Each birth celebrated, each death mourned
—and, in between, each life exalted.*

Matin No. 1 (Heroin Addict)

Filtered through dust clearing out and mist
burning off, light falls on empty birdhouses
and ghostly sedums, ambitious spider webs
and the glad-hand leaves of grapes. It dapples
sunchokes and hollyhocks and the brick fractals
of a middle school wall. It passes through holes
in an army-green shade, unravels into filaments
not unlike the white emetic strands of milkweed
and finds her in her bed, her skin picked over,
her hair tied into a length of rope, her panties
torn along the elastic band, her little boy bird-eyed
and smelling of urine: she's late for work again
and in her sleeping eyes it fathers a tiny panic.

Matin No. 2

With the morning's bird calls comes a woman's sobbing
that asks anyone who hears it to reconcile sympathy
with helplessness and speculate on first causes. My guess:

loneliness—no longer compromised, no longer comforted
—has finally found its voice. It ends when the chickadee
ends its two-note lament and the dove its hollow moan,

when people are already leaving for work and she's either
among them or in bed listening for fragments of her song
in a mockingbird's revised parody of how a day begins.

A Solitary Plum and a Line from *Paterson*

You left me the last and sweetest,
an Italian plum, a warm blue egg
of summer, white-dusted in a white
bowl; and even after I eat it it can
never be eaten and even after you
replace it it can never be replaced,
so long as one of us agrees to hear
the present pouring down: the roar, the roar of the present
—the wind's thin hiss, an oriole's
approval, a lawn mower's complaint:
accompaniment to a trifle of love
and now love's fixed, abiding song.

Death, Cocktails, St. Kitts

She's the poem the island recites and its sole
reassurance of life and process in the oceanic void.

She's the aria in the prevailing winds, the continuo
in the spin of stars, the rattle of happy-hour ice

at high tea when the canapés must be like sunny
radiations and the vodka very very cold. She smells

of coconut oil and Luckies and as she removes her
sandal awkwardly, carelessly, charmingly, like Nike

at the Acropolis, she teases the Brits for being
so woefully pale before becoming so painfully pink,

then proclaims that the well-traveled are everywhere
disliked: vistas scenic, children marasmic, how ironic

that the people they so diligently seek out
are the ones who never go anywhere.

For D., Who Enjoyed Reading Mystery Novels

She can drink, smoke, eat rich food:
it doesn't matter much any more;
but all she wants to do is read mysteries.
Maybe they distract her from the wall
the windowlight has become; maybe
only murder can keep her mind off dying.

I put on music she once knew how to play;
I bring her tea and it turns cold at her side.
Then a waiter notices that the only thing
breathing at Dr. A.'s table is the wine;
and it begins all over again: the search to find
whatever has been put there to be found.

Barfly Briefly Noted

In memory: T.J.

You spoke of lonely women,
plump as doves, who giggled
at your way with words (and

them). You performed
your bar tricks with olives
and for a shot of J&B a racy

limerick or to be or not to be
or what a piece of work is man.
When they found you dead in

your tub like Marat (and with
your uppers out!) everything
went down the toilet.

Now no one knows
the words to songs
or the meanings of words

or poems by heart. All we get
are crude jokes crudely told
or the silence of your grave.

Raising Children in Time of War (1943, 1967, 2003)

Monkeys say be extra careful and extra
alert: their moths are as large as our
pillowcases, their stars are all wrong

and their water flushes down toilets
the wrong way. Water-babies tell us how
lucky they are having no blood to bleed,

while juncos in their snug tuxedos say children
everywhere are disappearing, leaving behind
carnations of pink and turquoise smoke.

Mornings are like whales, gray without relief;
by noon, the news is almost always reassuring,
followed by songs almost always about love.

Mad Song

For my sister

She says there are holes in the light,
fissures that, opening to the past,
are born to collapse: laughing faces

from childhood, conversations that
reach an apex of ruddy intensity,
then suddenly end. She calls them *alberts*,

after our brother, who also comes
and goes, an annual visit, a few words
on the phone about this life ended

and that life revived by expectations,
a roundup of the news that never fails
to entertain. He's a comfort to her:

after all, aren't the stars only holes
in the night sky and when the past
is shared doesn't that make it true?

Americanization of a Poem by Wislawa Szymborska

No one in my family ever wrote a poem.
My father's laughter, because it was so rare,
was a kind of poetry, as was my mother's

acceptance of everything ordinary and out of luck.
The broken embrace of a cousin, once a boxer,
was never exempt from pain because of nights

spent in pursuit of a string of words. We speak
in a language that's mostly holes anyway
and so we say in a thousand different ways

that we work without getting rich, that we fall
into old age as an acrobat falls from a trapeze,
that we fight wars in remote places where

flies are the size of Windsor knots and yet
we only smile when we see each other with our
grandchildren who look like us all over again.

Senior Citizens without Air

Do you think the earth has lost its atmosphere, Willie?
—Samuel Beckett

Mockingbirds no longer pinwheel
across our backyards and our lindens
are much weaker in their applause.
At the bus stop, we exhale into
something that's more and more
like nothing at all and what we say
tends to die stillborn on our lips.
There's a noticeable lack of music
and fire. We turn green, patinas
along the exposed edges of things,
and blue, reduced to searching for air.
Breath spills into space and with it
go our stories and our warnings.
We're palpable angels, masses of
vapor, inhabitants of both heaven
and earth—now that the one
has become the other, so to speak.

The Wisest Aunt, Telling the Saddest Tales

1

They give her lunch, prick her finger for sugar.
Her stories are usually about being unlucky:
a young soldier is given away by the steam
from his own urine and so on and so forth.

2

During the war it was easy to find piecework;
after the war, it rained the names of the dead.
On her place mat is a map of the world: Canada
is a pink peony pressed into the northern seas.

3

She was the last to hold her daughter's hand;
death entering her had the sting of nettles.
When she was eleven she saw a boy's head
crack like an egg and a gray yolk spill out.

4

A phoebe builds its nest under an awning,
sky-blue and cloud-white stripes like her robe.
Once, against regulations, her son brought
her strawberries: O how delicious they were.

5

In the TV room, *Search for Tomorrow* is on,
the volume too high, the color all wrong.
How can you search for something that's
certain to arrive and just as certain to pass?

What I Know about Epistemology

For John and Vanessa

As the light goes, go. Be the rustling in the grass,
the fall from convention's good graces: learn,
or someone will have you filing files
or writing writs or demonstrating cutlery
or selling wisdom door to door.

Someone might even drop your lovely lives
into a factory and have you derusting rings
on the coolant-drenched turntable of a vertical lathe.
It's best for everyone that what you think you know
is generally thought of as general knowledge,

the kind you find in pool rooms and roadside bars,
in meadows as inviting as beds, in bedrooms
where it whispers like a ribbon untying,
sometimes even in universities; the kind
that's dangerous and inescapable and exact

down to every atom of everything there is,
to every name each thing goes by
and every law each thing obeys; the kind
that quietly accumulates until you end up
knowing more than you know.

Azaleas; or, What the Young Don't Know about Love

For Denise

Young couples spend their nights in large
showy houses learning what to say to
and where to touch one another, convinced
that we long for the sweetness age has sucked
out of our lives and the howl of hot sausage
the more timid rumble of bran and flaxseed

and prunes has replaced. They think we live
at the roots of their azaleas, a shifting of bones,
a kind of fertilizer. First blossoms bring bees
and scenes of love reenacted: what moves one,
the other won't deride; what one likes, the other can't
get enough of; what one dislikes, the other despises.

They have sex, taste salty; then sleep comes
and goes like a phantom. They say: *You know,*
there couldn't be such a thing as love
if there weren't such a thing as spring.
We say: *If love is undying,*
it has no need to be reborn.

NOTES

"French Lesson (*après* Larry Rivers)"
Inspired by a series of paintings by Larry Rivers known as
French Vocabulary Lessons.

Eh quoi! tout est sensible? is attributed to Pythagoras and
serves as the epigraph to "Golden Verses" by Gérard de
Nerval.

"The Hat City after Men Stopped Wearing Hats"
The Hat City is Danbury, Connecticut; the inauguration is
John F. Kennedy's; the poet is Robert Frost.

"What Her Door Said (after Catullus)"
Loosely based on "Poem No. 67" from *The Poems of Catullus,*
Peter Whigham, editor.

"A Solitary Plum and a Line from *Paterson*"
the present pouring down: the roar, the roar of the present
From William Carlos Williams' *Paterson*, Book Three, Part III.

"Death, Cocktails, St. Kitts"
like Nike at the Acropolis
The line refers to the relief known as "Nike Removing
Her Sandal," part of the parapet that surrounds the Nike
Temple at the Acropolis.

"Americanization of a Poem by Wislawa Szymborska"
Based on *"Pochwala Siostry"* ("In Praise of My Sister").

"The Wisest Aunt, Telling the Saddest Tales"
The title is from *A Midsummer Night's Dream,* II, i, 51.

About the Author

John Surowiecki is the author of *Watching Cartoons before Attending a Funeral* (White Pine Press, 2003), and five chapbooks: *Caliban Poems* (West Town Press, 2001), *Five-hundred Widowers in a Field of Chamomile* (Portlandia Group, 2002), *Dennis Is Transformed into a*

Thrush (White Eagle Coffee Store Press, 2004), *Further Adventures of My Nose: 24 Caprices* (Ugly Duckling Presse, 2005), and *Bolivia Street* (Burnside Review Press, 2006).

In 2006, Surowiecki won the Pablo Neruda Prize sponsored by *Nimrod International Journal* and finished second in the Sunken Garden Poetry Festival National Competition. In 2005, he was awarded a poetry fellowship from the Connecticut Commission on Culture and Tourism, Office of the Arts.

His publications include: *Alaska Quarterly Review, Antietam Review, Briar Cliff Review, Columbia, Cream City Review, Folio, Gargoyle, GW Review, Indiana Review, Kimera, MacGuffin, Mississippi Review, Nimrod, North American Review, Poetry, Prairie Schooner, Rhino, West Branch* and *Xanadu*. He is a graduate of the University of Connecticut where he received his B.A. and M.A. in English. As a student he won the University's annual Wallace Stevens Poetry Prize on two occasions. He makes his living as a freelance writer and is currently working on a long poem, *American Stroke.*

About the Artist

Robert Reichert received a B.F.A in art history at St. John's University in New York and went on to teach photography there upon graduation. He has also taught at the International Center of Photography and Parsons School of Design. Reichert's work has appeared in magazines such as *Life, Time, Psychology Today* and *Forbes*. Over the years, he has been commissioned by various Fortune 500 companies to take photographs for their annual reports and for advertising purposes. His personal work and portraiture has been exhibited widely and can be found in many private collections. He lives in West Hartford, Connecticut.

About the Washington Prize

The Hat City after Men Stopped Wearing Hats is the winner of the 2006 Word Works Washington Prize. John Surowiecki's manuscript was selected from among 304 manuscripts submitted by American poets.

FIRST READERS:
Cliff Bernier
Doris Brody
Mark Dawson
Deanna D'Errico
Angelyn Donahue
W. Perry Epes
Colin Flanigan
Elizabeth Hazen
Erich Hintze
Tod Ibrahim
Sydney March
Mike McDermott
Ann Rayburn
Jill Tunick
Doug Wilkinson

SECOND READERS:
Michael C. Davis
Brandon D. Johnson
Barbara J. Orton

FINAL JUDGES:
Karren L. Alenier
J.H. Beall
Sandra Beasley
Miles David Moore
Steven B. Rogers

About the Word Works

The WORD WORKS, a nonprofit literary organization, publishes contemporary poetry in collectors' editions. Since 1981, the organization has sponsored the Washington Prize, a $1,500 award to an American poet. Monthly, The Word Works presents free literary programs in the Chevy Chase Café Muse series, and each summer, free poetry programs are held at the historic Joaquin Miller Cabin in Washington, DC's Rock Creek Park. Annually, two high school students debut in the Miller Cabin Series as winners of the Jacklyn Potter Young Poets Competition.

Since 1974, WORD WORKS programs have included: "In the Shadow of the Capitol," a symposium and archival project on the African-American intellectual community in segregated Washington, DC; the Gunston Arts Center Poetry Series (Ai, Carolyn Forché, Stanley Kunitz, and others); the Poet-Editor panel discussions at the Bethesda Writer's Center (John Hollander, Maurice English, Anthony Hecht, Josephine Jacobsen, and others); Poet's Jam, a multi-arts program series featuring poetry in performance; a poetry workshop at the Center for Creative Non-Violence (CCNV) shelter; and the Arts Retreat in Tuscany. Past Master Class Workshops have featured Agha Shahid Ali, Grace Cavalieri, Thomas Lux, and Marilyn Nelson.

Since 1975, Word Works has published over 60 titles, including work from such authors as Deirdra Baldwin, J.H. Beall, Christopher Bursk, John Pauker, Edward Weismiller, and Mac Wellman. Currently, The Word Works publishes books and occasional anthologies under three imprints: the Washington Prize, the Hilary Tham Capital Collection, and International Editions.

Past grants have been awarded by the National Endowment for the Arts, National Endowment for the Humanities, DC Commission on the Arts & Humanities, Witter Bynner Foundation, Writer's Center, Bell Atlantic, Batir Foundation, and others, including many generous private patrons.

The WORD WORKS has established an archive of artistic and administrative materials in the Washington Writing Archive housed in the George Washington University Gelman Library.

Please enclose a self-addressed, stamped envelope with all inquiries.

The Word Works   PO Box 42164   Washington, DC 20015
editor@wordworksdc.com   www.wordworksdc.com

WORD WORKS BOOKS